Light Helps Me See

by Jennifer Boothroyd

first step nonfiction

Lerner Publications Company · Minneapolis

LERNER

SOURCE

Expand learning beyond the printed book. Download free, complementary educational resources for this book from our website, www.lerneresource.com.

The images in this book are used with the permission of: © Fuse/Thinkstock, p. 4, 5; ©iStockphoto.com/Lepro, p. 6; © iStockphoto.com/Daniel Bendjy, p. 7; © Todd Strand/Independent Picture Service, p. 8, 9 © Dragon Images/Shutterstock.com, p. 10; © iStockphoto.com/filmstroem, p. 11; © iStockphoto.com/cruphoto, p. 12; © Peshkova/Shutterstock.com, p. 13; © Elena Itsenko/Shutterstock.com, p. 14; © Toncsi/Shutterstock.com, p. 15; © iStock/Thinkstock, p. 16; © iStockphoto.com/tunart, p. 17; © Balic Dalibor/Shutterstock.com, p. 18; © Anemone/Shutterstock.com, p. 19; © Natalia Sannikova/Shutterstock.com, p. 20; © Iva Barmina/Shutterstock.com, p. 21; © 2xSamara.com/Shutterstock.com, p. 22;
Front Cover: © iStockphoto.com/Maica

Main body text set in ITC Avant Garde Gothic Std Medium 21/25.
Typeface provided by Adobe Systems.

Lerner Publications Company
A division of Lerner Publishing Group, Inc.
241 First Avenue North
Minneapolis, MN 55401 USA

For reading levels and more information, look up this title at www.lernerbooks.com.

Library of Congress Cataloging-in-Publication Data

Boothroyd, Jennifer, 1972- author.
    Light helps me see / by Jennifer Boothroyd.
        pages   cm. — (First step nonfiction. Light and sound)
    Includes index.
    ISBN: 978–1–4677–3911–5 (lib. bdg. : alk. paper)
    ISBN: 978–1–4677–4684–7 (eBook)
    1. Light—Juvenile literature. 2. Light—Properties—Juvenile literature. 3. Vision—Juvenile literature. I. Title.
QC360.B66 2015
535—dc23   2013040960

Manufactured in the United States of America
1 – CG – 7/15/14

Table of Contents

Why Do We Need Light?

How many dogs do you see?

Light makes it easier to see.

Now how many dogs do you see?

It is hard to see clearly in the dark.

Our **eyes** need light to see.

What color is this glove?

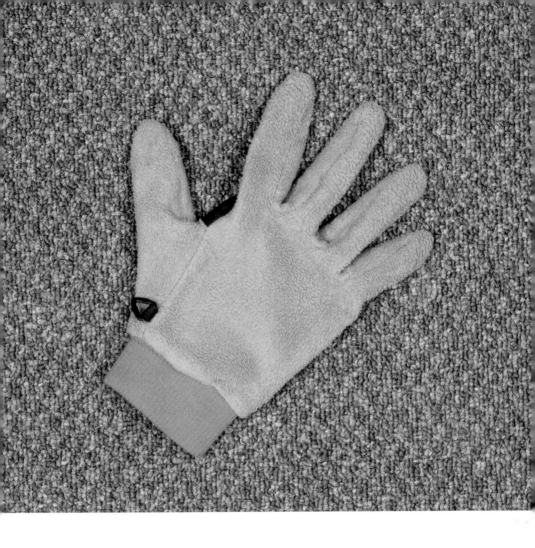

The glove is pink.

Our eyes need light to see colors.

Light comes from many places.

The sun gives off light.

A lightbulb gives off light.

Fire gives off light.

Light can pass through glass.

Sunlight shines through the window.

The curtains stop some of
the light.

Light **bounces** off things around us.

Our eyes catch the
bouncing light.

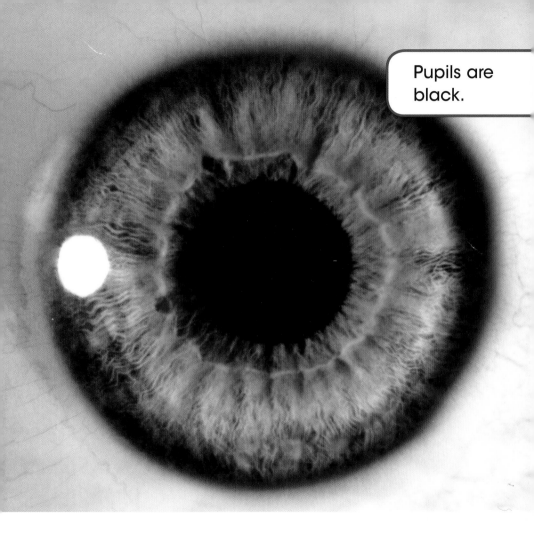

Pupils are black.

The **pupil** lets light into the eye.

The pupil gets small if the light is **bright**.

The pupil gets big if the
light is **dim**.

We need light to see.

Glossary

bounces – to fly around after hitting something

bright – giving off strong light

dim – giving off very little light

eyes – the body parts that sense light

pupil – an opening in the center of the eye that lets in light.

Index